THE ACT ACCORDINGLY SERIES

THINK

On Your

THOUGHTS

Volume II

DANIEL J. WILLIAMS

authorHOUSE

AuthorHouse™
1663 Liberty Drive
Bloomington, IN 47403
www.authorhouse.com
Phone: 833-262-8899

Published by AuthorHouse 10/18/2022

ISBN: 978-1-6655-7322-1 (sc)
ISBN: 978-1-6655-7320-7 (hc)
ISBN: 978-1-6655-7321-4 (e)

Library of Congress Control Number: 2022919231

Print information available on the last page.

Contents

Dedication

I give the glory to God for all that I do and have been able to do. After God I have to say that my mother Tracey A. Williams is directly responsible for me being the man I've become. I was not only taught well but I also got to witness my mother walk her talk.

My mother said to me, "You don't follow standards and meet standards. You set standards". You were always an encourager and a person who always spoke to the best in everyone and anyone. It is only right I follow in your footsteps.

Love You Much Tracey A. Williams

My Mother, Sister, Best Friend, Counselor, Business Mentor, and the Greatest example of a Holy Ghost Filled Disciple of Christ I've known. We're setting standards and not just reaching them!

Introduction

Think On Your Thoughts is not meant to be another thirty day devotional book of quotes or positive affirmations for daily excitement. The intention of this book is to have you identify belief systems, habits, and cycles that are placing a lid and ceiling of containment over your self-development and ability to enlarge your sphere of influence. Given the opportunity and the latitude to maneuver, what do you have an aptitude to be excellent in? Knowing that you have this natural genius within you means that you are in control of determining where to make your opportunity and you don't have to wait for permission, you hold the power of giving yourself the permission to be as excellent as you choose with your genius.

I want you to not be excited about a positive quote or affirmation but implement it and live it and not just be excited about the idea of it. I prefer that you correct incorrect habits and belief systems for you to be excited about the days of your life and not a day here and a day there. The more intentionality you direct towards what thoughts you think on will ultimately alter your decisions, your actions, patterns, habits, lifestyle, and your outcomes. Attempting to rearrange your circumstances will not change your trajectory. The thoughts you think on and the decisions you give animation to are the determiners of your trajectory.

Circumstances and lifestyles are a result of decisions whether made unconsciously or consciously. Recent studies suggest that on average most of us have 6.5 thoughts per minute and more than 6,000 thoughts per day. These thoughts range from, "I wonder what my dog is thinking right now?" to "I'm never going to be able to be good at _____?" to "God is so wonderful". Throughout a given day our thoughts will transition from being highly imaginative, to negative against ourselves or others, to life's enigmas, to being optimistic, and to thoughts of God's love.

Here's the thing: the thoughts that you capture and allow to resonate will end up being the direction of your thinking, behavior, and life. When you begin to entertain thoughts, be wise and really THINK ON YOUR THOUGHTS they form what you experience inwardly and outwardly.

DAY 1
Devotional

Don't close your eyes to see the dream again and again. Open your eyes to see what is required.

Proverbs 13:4
Good News Translation
No matter how much a lazy person may want something, he will never get it. A hard worker will get everything he wants.

A dream can only be dreamt once. We can always return to the memory of the dream but only have the dream once. Do not allow your dream to be a memory that you sneak away to revisit. Instead sew it and envision it vividly. Extract it from your imagination so that it becomes an experience that you live in. Stop rescheduling dates to live when your life is waiting for you to come join it.

Chapter one in the book of Genesis is probably one of the clearest examples of making it a reality I can offer you. God had an idea of this wonderful creation. He initially envisioned this creation. He then spoke aloud what he wanted to happen. God brought His creation into existence. Also in that same chapter one of Genesis mention was made of us being created in His image and in His likeness. That means that we are therefore replicas of God. Which also means we possess the capacity of imagining, speaking, and bringing our imaginations and thoughts into existence.

Possibilities remain possibilities as long we keep them confined to dreams. Be less excited about the dream and grow more eager to experience it and make it a memory. Stop thinking about it, stop talking about it, and pursue the tangibility of it.

#ActAccordingly

Don't close your eyes to see the dream again and again. Open your eyes to see what is required.

Proverbs 13:4
Good News Translation
No matter how much a lazy person may want something, he will never get it. A hard worker will get everything he wants.

When was the last time you delivered an intangible thing (a thought, an idea, or dream) into a tangible form (what can be experienced, seen, or touched)?

What's obstructing your creative force from developing the reality of your ideas? (START WITH YOU, BECAUSE ANY OTHER REPLY IS AN EXCUSE!)

For Example:

- Lack of initiative to start without someone else's prompting?
- Afraid that you just may succeed and have to keep succeeding?
- You don't trust that your ideas are worthy of being established?

Now that you've isolated the source of your obstruction, how do you intend to not be defeated by it another day?

(WHAT ARE YOUR STEPS TO GO FROM THOUGHT TO TANGIBLE?) For Example

- Purchase and designate a notepad to write that thought, idea, or dream
- Document what is required to establish moving from idea to tangible (Research)
- Outline how to implement the process of "Starting Day" to "Look at what I've done"

Create a binding agreement between the You that is in the process of creating

(the present you) and the You that is already experiencing the tangibility or experience of what you two brought to life.

(the future you)

Let him/her know you're on the way to joining them!

DAY 2
Devotional

Most of the darkest and most turbulent storms we encounter are usually self-induced. The same applies to our greatest peace, self-induced.

John 16:33
Amplified Bible, Classic Edition
In the world you have tribulation and trials and distress and frustration; but be of good cheer [take courage; be confident, certain, undaunted]! For I have overcome the world. [I have deprived it of power to harm you and have conquered it for you.]

Our moods are up to us and our choice. There may be external elements that work against the mood we choose, but our moods continue to remain our choice. There should be some decisions we make concerning ourselves that have a non-negotiable clause attached. Meaning I decided to always act in alignment with this and this alone. Christ preferred peace on a lake that had violent swirling winds and aggressive waves. Jesus preferred tranquil waters over raging ones so he made that announcement to the winds and the waves. The authority with which he spoke was recognized. Authority doesn't ask or say please. When a command from someone in authority and with authority gives a directive it is always done without resistance.

If you're not commanding an atmosphere of peace for _____ (Your Name Here) and firmly standing on that being the only acceptable criteria for you, then what happens is someone or something opposite of that criteria will decide the atmosphere that they want you in. The only constant in life that we absolutely have control over is our thoughts, our decisions, our reactions, and our responses. All other things, matters, or persons, aren't within our sphere of control and neither are we within theirs.

#ActAccordingly

DAY 2
Journal

Most of the darkest and most turbulent storms we encounter are usually self-induced. The same applies to our greatest peace, self-induced.

John 16:33

Amplified Bible, Classic Edition In the world you have tribulation and trials and distress and frustration; but be of good cheer [take courage; be confident, certain, undaunted]! For I have overcome the world. [I have deprived it of power to harm you and have conquered it for you.]

Emotions can assist the productivity of our day as well as disrupt the productivity of our day. We are in control of our emotions when we respond and misdirected by our emotions when we react.

Q: Which are you most frequently? One who responds or one who reacts?

Prematurely advancing in our emotions always leads to guilt, apologies, and having to return to our mistakes to perform corrective actions. Think about it. Am I wrong or dead on?

Q: At what point will you say, "Enough is enough, I keep losing this way? Today?

Since you said today is that day for you, PROVE IT. Do it now!

How? Place this reminder in your phone, on your whiteboard, or even a sticky note on the bathroom mirror or all over your house stating this:

IT ISN'T PEOPLE, OBJECTS, CIRCUMSTANCES, OR SITUATIONS THAT PROMPT MY DECISIONS AND PUSH ME INTO DOING ANYTHING.

THE CONTROL OR LACK OF CONTROL OF MY EMOTIONS ALLOWS ME TO WIN OR CONCEDE TO LOSSES.

Now repeat as often as necessary.

DAY 3
Devotional

If doing what needs to be done when it needs to be done seems uncomfortable - wait until it becomes an urgency.

Ecclesiastes 10:18
New King James Version
Because of laziness the building decays,
And through idleness of hands the house leaks.

Leisure has a tendency to look more attractive than work. Distractions usually receive priority while what should actually be priority receives neglect. Too often we find ourselves under pressure to produce what was required of us due to behaving in a nonchalant manner and showing little concern. Be honest with yourself. Am I calling you out on it? Projects at school? Deadlines at work? Bills sent out with the date of payment attached? The response is most often, "I've got time, I've got time", until the due date is a past due notice.

You'll continue to be a victim of being under pressure and consequences until you give your priorities priority over distractions. Leisure comes at a cost. However, that cost doesn't have to be expensive unless it's purchased before priority is first paid. Let's be clear about priority and leisure. This is the clarity, we do not "Work to play" but more like "Because of our work we can afford to play".

#ActAccordingly

DAY 3
Journal

If doing what needs to be done when it needs to be done seems uncomfortable. Wait until it becomes an urgency.

Ecclesiastes 10:18
New King James Version
Because of laziness the building decays,
And through idleness of hands the house leaks.

Let's place a focus on your most recent 6 months for this discussion.

- How many instances when you have had the finances to comfortably pay an obligation in advance you paid it?
- How many instances when you have had the finance to comfortably do so, instead of paying the obligation in advance you opted to make a self gratifying purchase?

How could the action of advance payment an asset to you?

Did the action of advance payment and gratifying purchase both place you in a winning position?

Absolutely correct! •*How did taking the action of that gratifying purchase prove to be more of a liability than an asset?*

Wise budgeting, issuing prompt payment, and practicing delayed gratification are acts of a wealth mindset.

Earning just enough to meet the requirements and issuing pay at the due date or during the

"Grace period" are acts of "Just enough to be completed". A survival mindset.

Which set of actions keeps you under the pressure of competing against due dates?

If you persist with actions that prove more problematic than beneficial, how do you intend to move to facilitate actions that are assets instead of liabilities?

DAY 4
Devotional

The view from the mountaintop is contingent on a climb.

Matthew 6:33
The Passion Translation
33 *"So above all, constantly chase after the realm of God's kingdom and the righteousness that proceeds from him. Then all these less important things will be given to you abundantly.*

The frustration we suffer in our efforts of achieving aren't always due to or connected to the process. In most instances it has nothing to do with the process at all. More times than few it is that familiar cliche, "PuttingThe Cart Before The Horse". Let's say there's a new athlete wanting endorsements, bonuses, and a championship ring. He wants all the benefits of champion status yet has not placed any focus into any of the preliminaries that are required. There's adopting the mindset and building the character of a champion. Champions train for excellence and not to be seen by an audience. Champions train as champions before they may be formally recognized as a champion. Lastly is the approach to each game. That approach is winning every game regardless to where they are in their season. It could be the opening, middle, or at the closing of the season and the thought is, "One game closer to winning the championship". "Win this game and I'm that much closer to a championship". Wanting a championship without those components, imagining is about as close as he'll get.

The same goes with spiritual matters. We should not expect to receive the fullness of God's promises when there's the absence of a consistent offering of our mind, heart, obedience, and true worship.

#ActAccordingly

DAY 4
Journal

The view from the mountaintop is contingent on a climb.

Matthew 6:33
The Passion Translation
33 "So above all, constantly chase after the realm of God's kingdom and the righteousness that proceeds from him. Then all these less important things will be given to you abundantly.

The purpose of GPS technology is for traveling a direct route to a destination. It announces only directions and possible dangers along the route.

Does your life's GPS have a destination in the input box? You sure? What's the present destination and ETA?

The screen shows certain establishments along the way yet it makes no mention to them. Why is that you suppose? Anything else minus dangers are insignificant to the intended destination?

Is your destination really a priority to you if you're intentionally taking detours (becoming distracted)?

You are aware that when you take time for the detour (distraction) you're pushing your arrival time back?

Destinations may remain in place until you arrive but how about the purpose of the destination? Will you still have time and access for the purpose of traveling or will you miss it?

It's no different with life and opportunities.

Are you aware that opportunities don't remain still waiting on our convenience to show up; they come with deadlines and expiration dates attached?

How often are you barely grabbing your opportunities and even worse by not making a priority of the opportunity you allow someone else to capitalize and you lose altogether? Is this still a pattern that needs correcting?

How can you begin to not find distractions attractive and stay deliberate about what should stay the priority?

DAY 5
Devotional

Success isn't simply about planning and then execution. Once you experience the vision, launch towards living it.

Proverbs 16:3
Put your works into the hands of the
Lord, and your purposes will be made certain.

Deadline, target date, 5 year plan, 90 day forecast. We have a compulsion with planning and announcing what _____ (Place Your Name Here) is going to make happen and going to do. Life is notorious for not always acting in agreement with what we believe should happen for us and the way we prefer it to happen. I believe the hugest "If" factor in any plan is other humans. Influencing other humans to cooperate when, how, and for as long as we need them to be for our successful outcome is a rare occurrence. An extremely rare occurrence. Remember the scripture [Jeremiah 29:11]? We may make plans but it's God's plans that are always flawless. That being said, always take into consideration [Jeremiah 29:11] any time you develop a desire to fulfill your own future prediction, be in relationship with any person, or on a quest to possess objects for yourself. Consult with God not _____ (Place Your Name Here) about what His desires and His plans are for you first. His plan clearly states He "Plans to prosper you not harm you". I don't believe anyone intentionally sets themselves up for failure, for heartbreak, or to be the victim of hardship. Yet it happens when we make plans and set sequences of events into motion.

Remember that next time you feel impatient or agitated with your plans. Once we begin to believe solely in what we know we often meet disappointment. Disappointment isn't a product of bad luck and it certainly does not come from God. Disappointment isn't even meant to be a part of our lives. Again remember [Jeremiah 29:11]. God has plans for what? Disappointment only becomes a part of our lives when we prefer our way. We can imagine our future but God has written our future.
#ActAccordingly

DAY 5
Journal

Success isn't simply about planning and execution. Once you experience the vision, launch towards living it.

Proverbs 16:3
Put your works into the hands of the
Lord, and your purposes will be made certain.

What would you credit as the greatest asset to your history of successes? For Example:

- Your attention to detail
- Your work ethic
- Your passion to always finish what you start

What would you credit as the greatest asset to your history of successes and how is it that you believe this asset contributes to your successes?

What in your opinion has been your greatest recurring hindrance to overcome in your history of missing the mark?

For Example:

- Procrastination or not acting promptly
- Overthinking the process
- Unable to acquire adequate resources

What in your mind has been your greatest recurring hindrance to overcome in your history of missing the mark and how do you believe you could rid yourself of this issue of missing the mark?

I intend to challenge your belief system today.

Truth is this, what you credit as your greatest asset isn't an asset at all but simply a quality trait. Nothing more than a tool to operate from. The only asset in your success history is God. He alone places sequences of events and persons in position to favor an outcome benefiting you. The truth about the hindrances to your missing the mark is that there are no multiple hindrances to list or consider but one. That hindrance is you. Yes you. You're your hindrance. It isn't that you're in God's way but that your desires are misplaced or your desires are for the incorrect reasons. Hence missing your mark.

In what two ways has this conversation altered your outlook on why events shift to your favor? In what two ways has this conversation altered your outlook on why events don't go in your favor?

The one consistency I've found throughout my life is that people will place blame on life and the devil for every inconvenience and uncomfortable situation.

Proverbs 28:13
Living Bible
A man who refuses to admit his mistakes can never be successful. But if he confesses and forsakes them, he gets another chance.

There are moments in life that are by design to happen and there are those other moments of life we ourselves trigger sequences of events. Mistakes are inevitable. Mistakes will be common occurrences within the experience of life. "You Live And You Learn" as the quote goes. There are those who learn from their mistakes and move forward. While there are also those who are repetitive in the same mistake until they create a cycle. A cycle is a loop of the same action again and yet again. Cycles impede and in no way will allow any positive progression. It's a loop! Round and round is the only direction!

Are you aware that not taking responsibility and placing blame is a sin? Yes, placing blame is a sin! Blaming is the equivalent of lying, bearing false witness, and attempting to conceal the truth. Again, yes God considers casting blame elsewhere a sin. Don't be alarmed and no need to panic. God isn't anxiously watching and waiting for the opportunity to condemn us or punish us for making mistakes. In fact, because of His omniscience God created an escape for us from shortcomings. It's a direct portal called Jesus for us to have access to grace, mercy, compassion, patience, and forgiveness. What's so wonderful about this is we don't even have to ask for it, just go to Him expecting to receive It because Christ already did the asking on our behalf. Forgiveness is already done. Our taking accountability keeps our mistakes from owning us. Taking ownership defeats embarrassment and allows us to dust off and recover from the mistake. No mistake remains permanent unless we avoid correcting it.

#ActAccordingly

DAY 6
Journal

The one consistency I've found throughout my life is that people will place blame on life and the devil for every inconvenience and uncomfortable situation.

Proverbs 28:13
Living Bible
A man who refuses to admit his mistakes can never be successful. But if he confesses and forsakes them, he gets another chance.

What is there about making mistakes that brings out this default response, "It wasn't me, it was"?

Would you agree or disagree that mistakes are indicators of a deficiency of experience in an area and not about incapability?

- If you do not agree, what would you determine as to the reason we make mistakes?
- If you agree, how could the acknowledgement of this be considered a positive?

What rating would you give yourself on your ownership of fault using a scale of 1 to 5?

1 being the lowest and 5 the highest.

Would you agree or disagree that where you rate says a lot to why you stay in familiar zones versus unfamiliar ones?

Or the reason you don't have reservations when it comes to approaching different experiences?

How much agreement would you lend to the idea that mistakes are how we learn our patterns for successful outcomes?

Much or little and why?

Ownership of our mistakes asserts our power over fear and blaming and doesn't create a hindrance to learn.

Write yourself a short reminder starting as such and conclude it tailored to you.

Place your name here is not exempt from making mistakes. The more I make, the more I learn. The more I learn the higher my probability of successful outcomes.

DAY 7
Devotional

The path to success is a "Clarity as you travel it" path.

Luke 17:14
Good News Translation
14 Jesus saw them and said to them, "Go and let the priests examine you." On the way they were made clean.

Positive progress. Changes for the better. Encouraging development. What these phrases have in common are that they all point towards improvement. The leapers followed Christ's instruction and started a sequence of events that led to they're healed conditions. First listening to Christ's instruction. Secondly believing that his instruction was credible. Lastly was their obedience to his instruction "Go" which led to their healing. They didn't exactly know how this was going to heal them but they believed that healing would happen as they walked. The principle of being obedient and following instructions for successful outcomes and progressive improvement can be implemented in parenting, business, athletics, and literally any pursuit of advancing to the next level. The Kingdom of God has set instructions in place for us to acquire not only spiritual but earthly favor and benefits but eternal as well. Instructions are like coordinates to a location. Follow the coordinates and you'll arrive at your intended location. Listen to the GPS and you'll arrive at your desired location.

The need to know full disclosure could actually end up becoming a deterrent rather than helpful in some journeys to accomplishment. Can you recall a journey that added character and maturity to you while on the way to your destination? Would you have gone forward if you knew you would have to be obedient to a "What's best for you" moment over having it according to your preference? That's the reason why just going sometimes without all the questions being answered is best. You can't and will not mature, develop, and evolve into your optimal self if you always know what's next.

#ActAccordingly

DAY 7
Journal

The path to success is a "Clarity as you travel it" path.

Luke 17:14
Good News Translation
14 Jesus saw them and said to them, "Go and let the priests examine you." On the way they were made clean.

What makes a painting a beautiful painting is it the bringing a vision to life, the passion in the strokes, the blending of the colors and shades, or is it the embodiment of all?

How could the approach to the process and our attitude contribute to dictating the outcome of the painting?

How often have you opted out of opportunities because you only had partial data to go forward with?

(Note I didn't say "No data")

On average which has presented you with better results? Access to all the details prior to beginning or when you only received partial details and you still proceeded?

How frequently do you deviate from instructions believing in yourself rather than the manufacturer?

- If it's rare, why do you trust the instruction manual?
- If it is frequent, do you perform the task in a more proficient timeline than the manual forecasts or does your way prolong the process and why do you believe this occurs?

Do you believe that the middle holds higher importance over an outcome than the beginning? Why or why not?

In what ways could your imagined outcome be altered by the middle part of a process?

The finish line is an indicator of completion but how you arrive is determined in the process. How can you make the process a priority?

DAY 8
Devotional

Stop placing all your focus towards the finish line. Knowing how to finish is more important than just wanting to finish.

Proverbs 16:3
Commit your work to the Lord and your plans will be established.

Weightlifting will without question give us strength, power, and a commanding stature. However, an athlete's training protocol isn't like that of a bodybuilder's. Bodybuilders don't weight train in the same manner that powerlifters train. Both methods utilize weight training but the training protocols differ because the intended outcome requires a specific preparation.

Another example would be the training protocol for a football athlete and a MMA fighter. I believe we immediately know there will be a difference in how these two athletes approach their weightlifting. The football athlete depending on his position will train for power, strength, and size. The MMA athlete will train for strength as well but also include more agility and endurance. There's certain demands each athlete's given sport requires of him to become recognized as a champion.

Our excitement to serve in our Father's kingdom is much the same. We all have to utilize the power of the Holy Spirit but our specific protocols will differ due to the specific purpose of our calling. This is why the Holy Spirit is our coach. He will guide us into our type of training, the frequency and intensity of our training, and also what we need to be fed for our type of training. Without the guidance and instructions on the "How To Move" within God's will and purpose for our assignments, it would be exhausting trying to fulfill those assignments.

The outcomes of our challenges will always be the evidence of how much consideration we gave to the preparation process.

#ActAccordingly

DAY 8
Journal

Stop placing all your focus towards the finish line. Knowing how to finish is more important than just wanting to finish.

Proverbs 16:3
Commit your work to the Lord and your plans will be established

Can you recount an instance of completing an assignment, competition, or activity that you walked away feeling ungratified rather than full of excitement with your accomplishment? What do you believe could have been attributed to those feelings?

Would you agree that it isn't the finishing or completion of actions that gratifies but the quality of the finish or completion that is the greater reward?

Consistent Focus + Consistent Aligned Actions = High Quality Outcomes

Sporadic Focus + Nonchalant Aligned Actions = Mediocre to Poor Outcomes

Choosing between the two formulas which defines you most accurately 85% of the time? Does the formula you chose leave you feeling content?

If not, how do you intend to recalibrate those sporadic actions to create consistent action towards High Quality Outcomes from today on?

DAY 9
Devotional

"That should be good enough" is a dangerous statement and an even more damaging habit to master.

Proverbs 18:9
Good News Translation
A lazy person is as bad as someone who is destructive.

Half done isn't finished. Three quarters isn't complete. At the finish line and not popping the tape isn't a victory.

What if Jesus had decided that the excessive abuse and criminal whipping he endured was all the blood he could give for our redemption? What if he decided to bypass dying on the cross? We wouldn't have received access to God's forgiveness, grace, or eternal life. "Being about my father's business" meant Jesus was under assignment and had a time restriction in which to render completed work to his Father. Redemption is a product of that completed work. Access to the Holy Spirit would not be possible for us without that death, resurrection, and ascension back to heaven from our Messiah Christ Jesus.

The completion of Christ's assignment carried heavy responsibility. It wasn't about him just finishing a task to say, "Done". It was about his work being completed because it was going to affect the lives of generations to follow.

Think of any of the many things you're responsible for completing. Does it affect you alone or will others also benefit or experience a loss depending on the quality of your effort? Someone is always in need of our assignment being completed and not just done.

#ActAccordingly

"That should be good enough" is a dangerous statement and an even more damaging habit to master.

Proverbs 18:9
The Message
Slack habits and sloppy work are as bad as vandalism.

How often have you ever been satisfied with mildly warm food being served to you in a restaurant?

Would you have an issue with a painter only painting the portion of your house he could only reach from the ground and no higher?

If you find it unacceptable from someone else to offer you subpart and mediocre why then do you present yourself and offer it to others?

Do you subscribe to the idea that there is some distinguishing difference between your mediocrity and someone else's mediocrity that makes yours more acceptable?

What would that difference be?

No matter what we do whether it be from a posture of excellence or from the posture of mediocrity it affects others. Don't believe it. Think of the last person who surprised you with some gesture of kindness. Now think of the last person who surprised you with a gesture of untrustworthiness.

- Did you respond the same to both gestures?
- Being able to prefer, which would prefer most and prefer least?

Are there any practices of habits that you could perhaps restructure that would place you as most preferred rather than least preferred by others?

- List 5 of your habits needing restructuring that would not only enhance you and your world but would prompt others to want to include you as a part of theirs as well.

(Do this reevaluation every 90 Days)

DAY 10
Devotional

The moment you stop being yourself and begin seeking to belong is the moment you begin suffocating under false identities.

Galatians 5:1
Good News Translation
Freedom is what we have—Christ has set us free! Stand, then, as free people, and do not allow yourselves to become slaves again.

Being accepted by the "Cool Kids" will have you doing what is outside of your character to be accepted. However, it isn't the group that is enslaving us but rather the idea of **"I Need To Be"**. The idea of inclusion is what ends up owning us. This misplaced need to be accepted then clashes with our authentic self. Before long we are lost in an identity we no longer want to continue but now we're too afraid to remove the mask. We settle for being what keeps us accepted rather than saying this isn't me. I would say this sounds very much like sin?

The beginning of a sin is exhilarating and appears to be something we can put on and take off as we wish. Eventually what sin does is breach the original agreement and starts making demands. Demands that turn what was part-time into a full-time obligation. What was a sneak away to enjoy some fun transitioned into a hostage situation.

God however doesn't bully us into any decisions and activities. What He prefers is to be chosen so that we always want for us what He wants for us. [Jeremiah 29:11] The reason God sent Christ to live among was to defeat sin and Satan by giving us a lifestyle blueprint to follow. Christ's sacrifice of himself, him being resurrected, and ascending back above the heavenly places was a ransom demand met for our freedom. The freedom of not being under manipulation, shame, or facing a penalty of eternal spiritual death.

There is a choice between being under restraint and walking in freedom.
#ActAccordingly

DAY 10
Journal

The moment you stop being yourself and begin seeking to belong is the moment you begin suffocating under false identities.

Galatians 5:1
Good News Translation
Freedom is what we have—Christ has set us free! Stand, then, as free people, and do not allow yourselves to become slaves again.

When does portraying what we believe people want us to be become a danger to who we are authentically?

What would you consider an indicator that we are losing ourselves?

How many circles of friends do you belong to that know you their way and yet another circle knows you their way?

How often have you avoided your different circles because you didn't feel up to being the character they know you as that day or moment?

Why do you continue the charade if it is tiring?

How is being afraid that the genuine you is too much or too little for certain circles unhealthy for your self esteem?

Inclusion and acceptance are not the equivalent of being welcomed.

Which is truly most important to you being in the company of friends or in the presence of people?

When you're giving up yourself to be accepted you don't grow.

Make a pact with yourself from this moment forward stating, "When I give up any part of myself that it will only be for my improvement and never for the loss of acceptance.

DAY 11
Devotional

There will always be unaccounted for variables between the distance of the beginning and the intended conclusion.

Psalm 37:7
Good News Translation
Be patient and wait for the Lord to act;...

We have a tendency to think that only our new endeavors are the ones sprinkled with unknown and unseen variables. We gravitate too much towards resting in a posture of "I've got this with my eyes closed" in regards to activities we've performed time and time again. Then the day appears when there is an interruption in the pattern we're accustomed to. A glitch in our matrix. What's our answer? We immediately go to our default reaction. Which is what? To force everything we know to remain in the pattern we recognize. "I've done this too much to not know what I'm doing", is our first thought. Frustration then drives us to repeatedly attempt to force our will onto the matter. What we have known and grown familiar with to be our winning formula has begun to stand as opposition to the plans that God has established prior to our believing that we know what's best for _____(Your Name Here). This is the reason for God's tap on the shoulder and reminder that it is He that positions our successes and not our delusion of "I've got this figured out."

Is God only "The God Who Can Do The Impossible" when life's level of difficulty is above our pay grade? Is He no longer that same God that we trusted for above and beyond what we could ask or think? [Ephesians 3:20]

Try to remember this. It is God alone who disperses and matures our talents, our gifts, our anointing, and every resource distributed for our use. We can plan and hope for the beat while God only has to speak it and it shall be so. Expect that the unexpected will happen as far as we are concerned but God never has moments of, "I didn't see that coming."

#ActAccordingly

24

There will always be unaccounted for variables between the distance of the beginning and the intended conclusion.

Psalm 37:7
Good News Translation
Be patient and wait for the Lord to act;...

How do you feel about the term "Self-made"? A prideful boast or a positive proclamation of accomplishment?

Can we agree that Success isn't a tangible object we can manipulate but we must come into agreement with it in order to experience it?

Would you agree or disagree that a culmination of appropriate actions done at the appropriate times leads to meeting with success, not creating success?

Agree or disagree? Success comes from a collaboration of agreements whether indirectly or directly?

- An agreement with someone's prior research and information
- An agreement with someone's advice on necessary resources for necessary actions

A boxer defeats opponents in the ring by the power of his hands but not without the assistance of a training team. Advisors that provide him access to creating appropriate mindset, appropriate skill set, and instructions towards success. Agree or disagree?

- The sport recognizes the boxer as accomplishing great things but is he "Self-made"? Did he by himself become champion?

Humility and acknowledgement of others is one of the more powerful keys to success. God honors humility and people respond more positively to humility.

It takes little to blur the thin line between taking pride in what you do and who you are and pridefulness which crosses into misplaced self-confidence.

"I'm Self-made. I built what I have from my own sweat and blood" or "I've worked hard to accomplish what I'm experiencing but I couldn't have done it alone".

- Knowing that wording is vital when communicating which statement do you believe would invite and which would repel?

If you needed an adjustment in mindset and communication to position you to accomplish more, what would that look like for you?

DAY 12
Devotional

Earthquake resistant structures are reinforced to continue standing due to the ability to redistribute the vibrations that would normally cause its collapse.

Colossians 2:7
New Life Version
Have your roots planted deep in Christ. Grow in Him. Get your strength from Him.

Christ gave warning to his disciples and to us that there will be adversities of this world that would find us. Both from the natural realm as well as the spiritual. Prior to the Holy Spirit we had belief systems that rested upon slowly eroding foundations. What were those foundations? Looking to ourselves, putting expectation in others, and seeking gratification from objects or experiences are those eroding false foundations. Our appetites and choices of excitement are frequently changing. People's likes and dislikes towards us are always shifting. Disappointment usually comes alongside having misplaced faith. Scripture uses the description of sinking sand in an illustration. (Matthew 6:27)

Then there's the stability of placing faith in God. Not choosing Him first, but God being our "Without question!". There is no shelf life with any part of God! No part of Him is inconsistent and varies. Our God is faithful and our God is Faithfulness. You aren't reading a grammatical error. I said our God is Faithfulness. He doesn't have to practice being what He is. He is as powerful today as He was yesterday and the moment before he spoke time into existence through eternity. In that warning about there being adversities in life, there was also a message of assurance attached. "But take hope! I have power over the world!"[John 16:33]

#ActAccordingly

DAY 12
Journal

Earthquake resistant structures are reinforced to continue standing due to the ability to redistribute the vibrations that would normally cause its collapse.

Colossians 2:7
New Life Version
Have your roots planted deep in Christ. Grow in Him. Get your strength from Him

When was the last time you began anything with absolute excitement only to abandon it just as quickly?

What was the honest reason for the abandonment of your idea?

Are you led by a "Let's just see what happens", an "I can do that too", or an "I can do that too and better" mindset?

How did you develop this mindset and what continues to influence it?

When you have a choice of choosing products or services which is your preference and why is that your preference?

A.   A Good Product or Service

Or

B.   An Excellent Product or Service

Are you the rating of the product and service you prefer and if there is a difference – why is there a difference and what's your strategy for upgrades and enhancements?

DAY 13
Devotional

The prayers we pray when there is no storm are those prayers that shield us once we do encounter a storm.

Colossians 4:2
Easy-to-Read Version
Never stop praying. Be ready for anything by praying and being thankful.

We don't tend to think of our prayers as being deposits or investing. When you make deposits or invest, you're placing it there for future use or a future return. Most often when we pray we're in anticipation of immediate results. So it's safe to say we tend to frequent the bank for making more withdrawals than deposits. When we make an investment we prefer a quick return rather than a prolonged wait.

Isn't the purpose of a savings account or an investment portfolio done for the sole purpose of future security? There's a sense of relief in knowing that when an unexpected expense surfaces there are finances readily available to cover the costs. Reviewing the growth of an investment or investments offers a sense of security that our retirement fund or world cruise nest egg will be available as predicted.

Think about it. The more of ourselves we give to God then the more we see God's hand in the matters and concerns of our lives. I'm speaking about quality of life. I'm speaking of having a Jeremiah 29:11 outlook.

What God appreciates from us most is our consistent pursuit of His ways. Our consistent pursuit of fulfilling what He has assigned to us. Our consistent pursuit of His presence. Our consistent adoration and worship of Him. Our faithfulness, our prayer, our fasting, our worship, our obedience are the deposits we make but it's our committed consistency that determines the ROI (Return on investment) that we receive.

#ActAccordingly

The prayers we pray when there is no storm are those prayers that shield us once we do encounter a storm.

Colossians 4:2
Easy-to-Read Version
Never stop praying. Be ready for anything by praying and being thankful

Why would someone who cannot swim feel a higher measure of safety wearing their life jacket around the boat as opposed to just having it conveniently placed nearby?

Do you believe a methodical person holds an advantage over a person who has an "I'll cross that bridge when I get to it" mindset? Why or why not?

There are many who see only a need to prepare for the "What if" and those who only see the
"Everything will work out" type of lenses.

- Which are you and how did you come to choose this lens that you view life through?

How could being a hybrid of "What if" and "Everything will work out" be an advantage while being only one or the other a handicap?

How do you view prayer?

- As a contingency? Why?
- Done only in a time of need? Why?
- For every activity and every moment?

Which of those choices matches your prayer life presently and what are you implementing to solidify consistency in an upgraded version of that?

DAY 14
Devotional

False starts work against you and not for you.

Isaiah 45:2
Good News Translation
"I myself will prepare your way, leveling mountains and hills. I will break down bronze gates and smash their iron bars.

Until a book is read in its entirety the author remains the only one with any knowledge of the ending and plot twists of that story. If we read ahead we'll be disadvantaged. We would be at a loss as to the hows and the whys leading to the chapter we decided we would rather skip ahead to. When we are viewing the steps regarding a diagram and skip directly to the finished product page we miss the procedures of the assembly process. While the ending is important to know, there is an order of importance that must be followed to properly get to the end. Anxiousness always results in having to backtrack to the portion we tried skipping over to arrive at a premature conclusion. There is a reason for the order of beginning, middle, and ending.

God has written our stories and has framed the sequence of events to match a perfect conclusion. [Jeremiah 29:11]

God's creation shows time and again His attention to detail, the absence of flaw, and that He is consistently reliable. The account of Creation in Genesis chapter one is evidence of the importance of performing everything within a designated order.

#ActAccordingly

DAY 14
Journal

False starts work against you and not for you.

Isaiah 45:2
Good News Translation
"I myself will prepare your way, leveling mountains and hills. I will break down bronze gates and smash their iron bars.

[In sports, a false start is a movement by a participant before being signaled or otherwise permitted by the rules to start.]

In football, the offensive team (team with the ball) loses 5 yards due to a false start. In track, the runner's false start stops the race and requires starting over again?

False starts usually occur due to hyper anticipation of the signal to proceed ahead. How many life experiences from this past 6 months are you able to relate to this sports reference of premature action?

Did you step back to reset and restart or did you just walk away altogether?

The way you respond to your restarts after a false start greatly determines the type of progress you'll make from that restart. Do you become more critical of yourself and delay restarting or do you look for the lesson and immediately return to the task at hand?

Why would being critical be worse than starting over?

How does dusting off and resuming keep momentum on your side?

There are also those who never go to their line over the fear of making a false start. How often has overthinking caused you to run away from opportunities?

How often are you standing in paralysis suffering from the "But how will I know when it is the right time" question. Keep in mind that no movement is actually worse than making a mistake. You get to learn from mistakes, adjust and then make positive progress. It isn't possible to learn how to move forward and maneuver from a position of inaction.

Don't view the penalty of having to restart as a punishment. When you view it, view it as a free pass to insight. Now you know what to expect, giving you an advantage of moving with even more calculated execution.

Let yourself know that from this day forward that <u>Your Name Here</u> mistakes can actually be more of a support than disadvantage. I will from this point <u>finish according to your need of change</u>.

DAY 15
Devotional

Running towards the easy and comfortable choice often becomes a cage with the illusion of that comfortable becoming the lock that keeps us prisoner to that very cage.

Proverbs 24:33-34

The Passion Translation

33–34 Professional work habits prevent poverty from becoming your permanent business partner. And: If you put off until tomorrow the work you could do today, tomorrow never seems to come.

Tools left unused will obviously rust at a more expedient rate than those that are being used more often. The tool being unused for periods of time doesn't make it inadequate for future use. In fact, it doesn't become inadequate at all. It only needs to be utilized in the capacity in which it was created for. The evidence of an undone task is clear evidence of neglect. Neglect isn't not being equipped to perform a task. Neglect is being equipped and responding with dereliction of duty or responding in a nonchalant manner towards accomplishing that task. When productive results are not seen, that's when the excuses begin to surface. Blame becomes the default answer to "What happened?". Avoidance of taking ownership for the non-fulfillment of duties becomes the primary activity instead of a sequence of corrective actions.

The idea of "I've got time" or "Tomorrow" are the largest contributors to unrealized dreams, purpose, and the collapse of unmet potential. The time to do anything after it is presented to us is the time of "Now".

#ActAccordingly

DAY 15
Journal

Choosing the path of least resistance eventually becomes a habit of settling for the bottom.

Proverbs 24:33–34
The Passion Translation
33–34 Professional work habits prevent poverty from becoming your permanent business partner. And: If you put off until tomorrow the work you could do today, tomorrow never seems to come.

A 5AM fitness session at the gym or 5AM start time for a weekend getaway? Why would you go to bed with more excitement for one over the other?

What's your pattern when it comes to tasks?

1. Are you one who immediately goes for the simplest tasks first in attempts to avoid the more difficult? Why is this your pattern?
2. Are you one who competes with them self in raising their level of performance so you'll seek the more difficult tasks first? Why is this your pattern?

I've found that those who bore easily aren't comfortable in repetitive activities.

If I was able to monitor you for 30 days would I come to the conclusion that you're predictable or that you aren't one that does well with being confined to patterns?

- In either case how would you validate your repetitive nature or not so repetitive nature? Why do you do it the way that you do it?

Would you agree or disagree that before you can be considered efficient, excellent, or a success within an area that a pattern of disciplines would need to be established first?

Are you willing to promise yourself that this will be your new character trait? Go ahead, write the promise to yourself. Write it now.

DAY 16
Devotional

Self-development is devotion to the decision of progressive change until the progressive change.

Ecclesiastes 7:8
Contemporary English Version
Something completed is better than something just begun;...

A team that starts with the best record in the NFL doesn't receive the same level of attention as the Super Bowl champions.

The runner who began a race with great stride and distanced themselves doesn't receive First place recognition if that stride and distance from the remaining group isn't from start to finish.

2 Kings chapter five gives an account of a military commander named Naaman who seeked healing from the prophet Elisha. Naaman was directed to dunk himself seven times in the Jordan River to cure his leprosy. This military commander's healing had a single requirement. That requirement was to follow through with the completion of seven dunks in the river to be healed. Any dunks less than seven would not be enough for his healing. Naaman's being cleansed of leprosy was the end result he expected to receive at the end of his journey to see the prophet. To possess what we say we want will always require more than just wanting it badly. It requires wanting it and doing the necessary until possession. Once we initiate motion towards "It" there must be a momentum towards "It" until we reach "It". The strength of a positive obsession usually determines the passion involved in the pursuit.

#ActAccordingly

DAY 16
Journal

Self-development is devotion to the decision of progressive change until the progressive change.

Ecclesiastes 7:8
Contemporary English Version
Something completed is better than something just begun;...

Have you ever attended an awards or recognition ceremony for someone who didn't achieve anything but had the intention to?

Can't say that I have either.

There is usually always an underlying dynamic that fuels our purposes and keeps us on a task until its best completion.

What's that single dynamic that keeps you returning to a task until its best completion?

Which is closest to accurate about why you normally abandon tasks either prematurely or gradually?

- Lack of daily excitement or frustration from your efforts going unrecognized or going unacknowledged by those you feel should be doing so?

Uncertainty can be a bridge or it can be a chasm. It can be an invitation to some and a repellent to others.

Does your preference lean towards accepting challenges or turning and walking away from what may require more effort than easy does it?

Why is that and what has shaped your personality this way?

Promise yourself that you'll stop choosing abandonment over gaining advantages. That instead of words of explanation you'll be an action verb.

Talkers and quitters aren't achievers or finishers. You can't be both.

DAY 17
Devotional

Abandoning unproductive practices will be difficult. The establishment of beneficial practices will be difficult. One carries a burden while the other allows freedom.

2 Corinthians 10:4
Good News Translation
The weapons we use in our fight are not the world's weapons but God's powerful weapons, which we use to destroy strongholds.

Thoughts are passing ideas. Some thoughts we allow to vanish. Other thoughts we allow to stay and expand. Once direct attention is given to a thought our mind begins to recall related information we've received and any past experiences to validate the same. The more our mind continues to seek validity for a thought the more that thought begins to mature into a belief.

Ideas become thoughts and thoughts become beliefs and beliefs can potentially become sanctuaries or they can become prisons. Both of these structures are called strongholds. However, the original purpose of a stronghold was for protection and concealment from attacks. Satan however constructs his strongholds for the purpose of imprisonment from The Truth of God. Satan's only agenda is the more he can convince us to believe in his lies the more we will view God's Truth as being the lie to not believe. God desires to be our protector and stronghold from the lies of satan because He (referring to God) is the only stronghold that cannot be breached or destroyed. (2 Samuel 22:3 - Psalm 18:2)

While there are strongholds for captivity there also remains a stronghold for freedom. All throughout the scriptures God communicates the message of do not fear, don't be afraid, or to worry about outcomes because with Him being our benefactor our outcome will always be satisfactory and then some.

Ephesians 3:20

The Passion Translation

Never doubt God's mighty power to work in you and accomplish all this. He will achieve infinitely more than your greatest request, your most unbelievable dream, and exceed your wildest imagination!

#ActAccordingly

DAY 17
Journal

Abandoning unproductive practices will be difficult. The establishment of beneficial practices will be difficult. One carries a burden while the other allows freedom.

2 Corinthians 10:4
Good News Translation
The weapons we use in our fight are not the world's weapons but God's powerful weapons, which we use to destroy strongholds.

Reflecting on past experiences, who would you attribute credit towards for your triumphs and what would you point to as the contributing element in your experiencing those triumphs?

I don't know you but would I be assuming correctly that your response was that you and a deliberate decision you made is why you experienced those triumphs?

Wonderful. Would you continue to agree with me that that first response should also be the identical response to if I formed the question in such a way to ask who and what would you say were the contributing factors in your less than triumphant experiences?

External forces cannot determine outcomes. Circumstances, sequences of events, and the decision of others not in agreement with our decision are excuses.

When you experienced your triumphs didn't you attribute the credit to you and your decisions? When you experienced the not so triumphant experiences were you forced to comply or did you make a decision to surrender to another decision outside of your own?

Close your eyes and reflect on an experience when you made a decision to accomplish a certain campaign and it happened.

As you proceeded in your campaign were all the necessary resources available to you upon your initial decision?

- While being deliberate in your campaign did the resources and sequence of events become accessible to you as you continued?

So would you agree with me that it takes you and your deliberate push forward for triumph and that anything less than triumphant equates to you and a decision of surrender?

In what way would you prefer the remainder of your life to be lived? Triumphant? Accomplished? Creating value? (Fill in your blank)?

Make a pact with yourself today that you will not comply with anything opposite of your preference. Anything opposite is surrender and surrender doesn't coincide with triumph and you cannot do it.

I'm ready" is evidence of prior preparation. A request for more time is the evidence of being unprepared.

Luke 9:61
Contemporary English Version
Then someone said to Jesus, "I want to go with you, Lord, but first let me go back and take care of things at home."

You didn't miss the opportunity. You were aware of the opportunity and didn't move on the opportunity before the opportunity closed. You assumed that the opportunity would remain open while you took your time. Opportunity doesn't wait for our indecisiveness or nonchalant attempts at action. There's a life span that comes attached to each opportunity. When we move promptly, we capture the opportunity's benefits. When we respond too slowly then we get closed off from that opportunity's benefits.

It may return or may not return. If it does return, it may not return with the same level of significance as it did when it made its original presentation. (**HINT: Take your opportunity when your opportunity makes itself available.**)

Opportunities are not a happenstance and always arrive aligned with our destiny.

Opportunity presents itself according to our willingness to move upon presentation. Ready doesn't have hesitation. Prepared doesn't need additional time.

#ActAccordingly

"I'm ready" is evidence of prior preparation. A request for more time is the evidence of being unprepared.

Luke 9:61
Contemporary English Version
Then someone said to Jesus, "I want to go with you, Lord, but first let me go back and take care of things at home."

What do you consider worse, someone dragging their feet to begin or the one unhurried to finish?

Why do you consider one worse than the other?

Does one of these personalities match you and why are you functioning with this personality? If neither personality is you then what is your personality type pertaining to the start and completion of matters?

"You Gonna Mildew or Barbeque"? When I first heard this question with it's jab at a person's procrastinate behavior I was immediately attracted to it.

You intend to "Mildew or Barbeque"?

You know what it is you're being lackadaisical towards. What are you going to do?

While waiting for the baton to be handed off a relay runner must be ready and positioned for the other teammate's approach to become a participant in the race.

Would you disagree with me that when there is a particular opportunity, not just any opportunity but that particular opportunity that we're waiting on we should be poised to hit the ground running when it approaches?

Why is this best to be poised this way?

Have you ever been found in the awkward moment of unpreparedness at the very moment preparedness was the most needed?

Have you had other similar moments preceding that? What changed or why did you continue this pattern?

Opportunities that you should be prepared for are the opportunities that you think on the most. Whatever is the "Your Opportunity" that you desire, be prepared for its emergence and to be "All In" once you assume the opportunity.

Promise yourself on this day that what you want you'll prepare for and what you're given you'll complete.

Start with "On this day (Today's Date) I (Your Name) will not just be prepared but will also conclude (Name The Task, Opportunity, or Objective)... The remainder is yours to complete.

DAY 19
Devotional

Power is functioning while aware of our strengths as well as our weaknesses.

Proverbs 4:12
Good News Translation
Nothing will stand in your way if you walk wisely, and you will not stumble when you run.

There are sports players who aren't just good players but natural athletes. There are the students who are just genius when it comes to deciphering information with clarity. These attributes are gifts God given abilities that don't require concentration. These attributes can lead a person to an arrogant disposition when a spirit of humility isn't coupled with that gifting.

It's due to pride that God places us in holding patterns from time to time. What I mean by a holding pattern is when it seems as if God isn't shifting things to our advantage or it seems as if He isn't even shifting us for that matter. This is never the case with God of course. He is afterall the omniscient God. As far as God's concerned it's more of a safety measure for our benefit. It's God's way of saving us from becoming a danger to ourselves. God knows us well, and what He knows is that He must take us through a character metamorphosis before every new level up season. Then when He releases us, He can trust us to be responsible with our new favor, new blessings of increase, promotion and status upgrade. Pride and vanity are extremely easy to walk into unconsciously. Once walking through that door and becoming comfortable it becomes ever so difficult to walk away from that behavior consciously. So the purpose of the holding pattern is for growth into matured humility. The maturity to distinguish between what's appropriate and what is reckless. We would do well to remember that it is God who is the Creator and we were crafted by His power and not our own. We didn't create for ourselves any of our gifts, talents, or above average abilities. We only grew to discover what was in us which means they were there before we knew they were there. Gifts, talents, and abilities can take us to many destinations but an inappropriate attitude will make it a return trip.

#ActAccordingly

DAY 19
Journal

Power is functioning while aware of our strengths as well as our weaknesses.

Proverbs 4:12
Good News Translation
Nothing will stand in your way if you walk wisely, and you will not stumble when you run.

blind spot (noun):
a tendency to ignore something especially because it is difficult or unpleasant

Would you ignore inflating a nearly flat tire before taking an out of town vacation just because you're in a hurry to get there?

Why?

How are making life decisions and vacation decisions similar?

Do you believe that weaknesses come as naturally as strengths and that both require your attention simultaneously?

If there was an exposed area in your security system would you leave it exposed? Why would you address the exposed area?

How frequently have you experienced the loss of relationships and/or opportunities as a consequence of neglecting that you have an area of weakness in expressing disagreement maturely, an inability to accept critique without offense, stubbornly receiving instruction, or (fill in your blank) because we each have different weaknesses deserving of our attention?

Do you prefer destructive patterns over progressive?

Would you prefer driving to Florida with four inflated tires or three inflated and one flattened? Why?

Your strengths don't require as much attention as your weakness but they do both require your attention for a higher level of performance.

What do you intend to do differently?

DAY 20
Devotional

It isn't the painting but rather the details in the painting that's most beautiful about a painting.

Proverbs 21:25
Common English Bible
The desires of the lazy will kill them, because their hands refuse to do anything.

Chapters, phases, and increments are all descriptives of a process for how anything and everything comes into existence. God created existence in six days. Each day required something being completed prior to the next day's creation being started. God could have simply said, "Let there be...", and established all of creation in an instance. Afterall, He is The Most High - God Almighty.

In my opinion, God wanted us to recognize that all things must have an order to them. When accomplishing or establishing anything there is a process to it. A first, second, next, and so on until completion.

Patience and working within a process is not one of the greater character traits of humans. Once we have seen and created a mental experience with whatever it is that appeals to us, we are then fixated. Our dominant thought is centered on possession. All other thoughts after that thought are, "And I want it now."

God created each part of creation a day at a time to ensure that what He did prior could support what He would do after. We must remember that each decision is being built on a last decision for a future decision to bring us to that tangible conclusion or experience. There isn't a most or more significant move to focus on. There's no such move as a most significant move. There is only every grain of sand until there is a beach. There is only every brush stroke until there is a painting.

#ActAccordingly

DAY 20
Journal

It isn't the painting but rather the details in the painting that's most beautiful about a painting.

Proverbs 21:25
Common English Bible
The desires of the lazy will kill them, because their hands refuse to do anything.

Work is that detail that cannot be excluded when there is an endeavor for the conception of anything of excellence. After the thought, the vision, and the planning comes the execution of the work.

Name the most current experience or new thing in your life that has you feeling proud beyond measure. Did you do any consistent work towards realizing this experience or ownership of what you now possess and why were you consistent in your pursuit?

Which truly means the most to you the experience, your ownership, or the fact that you are responsible for the existence of what is now bringing you joy and pride?

What was that detail that you implemented that has you positioned in this place of joy and pride?

Would you agree that work and effort are non-negotiables for the transference of our thoughts, desires, and plans from the intangible to tangible the unseen to seen?

Productivity and avoidance both require effort and energy. One places something new in your life and the other it doesn't just leave you as were but also in deficit.

Can you recall an instance when you avoided work and then a moment surfaced that you needed that same work you avoided to be done to move to secure an opportunity?

What disturbed you the most, missing the opportunity or that your laziness caused you to miss the opportunity?

Work isn't just work but the ingredients to create the whole, details to make the complete, or the sequences to bring the conclusion.

Will you as your present self always secure the best scenario for your future self to do the same for their future selves?

How do you intend to do this?

DAY 21
Devotional

Our errors, mistakes, and habitual habits are not final.

2 Peter 2:20

Good News Translation

If people have escaped from the corrupting forces of the world through their knowledge of our Lord and Savior Jesus Christ, and then are again caught and conquered by them, such people are in worse condition at the end than they were at the beginning.

We are in error when we don't have knowledge of what we're doing is wrong. We make mistakes when we've done something we know is wrong, but it was only done accidentally. We only become habitual offenders when we knowingly repeat what we know to not be a correct course of action.

Redemption clears away every error, mistake, and sin we unconsciously and we willfully choose to live in. What that means for us is that all of our sinful acts are forgiven and forgotten by God. It's the accuser of men - satan, that doesn't want us to live differently and forget our past.

1 Peter 5:8

Living Bible

Be careful—watch out for attacks from Satan, your great enemy. He prowls around like a hungry, roaring lion, looking for some victim to tear apart.

Rejoice when satan wants to remind you of the mistakes you made and the life you once lived. Rejoice? Yes, rejoice. You can rejoice because you no longer think as you thought, behave as you behaved, or keep the same social circles, or blindly follow the sound of culture's cadence. So rejoice because satan has only reminded you that just as Chtist overcame sin, death, and the grave, you have also done the same. No longer does satan have power over the person you are presently. He no longer has the capability to restrain you in isolation, guilt, and embarrassment because you now have liberty in Christ Jesus. You are now unchained to live freely within The KingdomofGod!

#ActAccordingly

DAY 21
Journal

Our errors, mistakes, and habitual habits are not final.

2 Peter 2:20
Good News Translation
If people have escaped from the corrupting forces of the world through their knowledge of our Lord and Savior Jesus Christ, and then are again caught and conquered by them, such people are in worse condition at the end than they were at the beginning.

Believe it or not the largest threat to progressive achievement is not Procrastination but rather an enemy called "Cycles".

cycle (noun)
a series of events or processes that is repeated again and again, always in the same order

Does this question sound familiar to you at all? "Why does this keep happening to me?"

I know it's familiar to me. I've repeated this very question at several stages of my life.

Now here's the real question: Was it life that was bullying me or was it (Place your name here) and my unwise decisions that kept me creating the series of repetitive experiences that I continued normalizing?

(Yes, you were suppose to be speaking in the 1ˢᵗ person) Which is your struggle? The unhealthy pattern or detaching from the unhealthy thing connected to the unhealthy patterns?

It took a series of decisions to get into this place therefore it will take a series of "Deliberate" decisions and actions to walk away from these unhealthy cycles and patterns. Notice I didn't say fix them, turn them around, or straighten them out I said walk away from. Walk away means leaving it where it is and you place distance between the two of you.

What does this look like for you?

DAY 22
Devotional

Taking care of Tuesday on Monday simply requires taking care of Monday all day Monday.

Matthew 6:34
New Life Version
Do not worry about tomorrow. Tomorrow will have its own worries. The troubles we have in a day are enough for one day.

Tomorrow is meant for tomorrow. When you stare at tomorrow too long you don't handle the day that's present.
[Matthew 6:11 (NLT)
Give us today the food we need]
The psalmist asked The Lord for his food for that day. He knew that the food that was supplied to him for that day was to strengthen and give him his vitality for the matters of that day. God continues to tell us in [Jeremiah 29:11] that he has a plan for prospering us. That we have a future to be excited about receiving. A future to be received and not made. Recognizing that God's plan is an active plan should be enough assurance to override any fears of "What if...".
Psalm 68:19

The Passion Translation

What a glorious God! He gives us salvation over and over, then daily he carries our burdens!
Pause. It isn't meant for us to approach our days with a "Try to face it and survive it" kind of mindset. Not when God desires for us to invite Him to walk with us in our day to day to ensure we experience the joys of each day that arrives. When we utilize what God has given us for that day during that day we've won not only that day but now know how to win the days to come.
#ActAccordingly

DAY 22
Journal

Taking care of Tuesday on Monday simply requires taking care of Monday all day Monday.

Matthew 6:34 Journal
New Life Version
Do not worry about tomorrow. Tomorrow will have its own worries. The troubles we have in a day are enough for one day.

Is it possible to satisfy a hunger you will experience for tomorrow's dinner with today's dinner? Exactly. Tomorrow has not yet arrived. The hunger has not yet arrived so it isn't possible for you to take care of tomorrow's issue until you have tomorrow's issue.

Excluding acting negligent with our responsibilities and certain details, another contributor to our unconscious sabotage on our attempts at positive progression is being fixated on the next move and ignoring the "First things first" moves waiting to be completed.

How often has this handicapped your pace to successful results?

What types of corrective actions do you believe you need for correcting a habit if unconscious sabotage?

What prompted the change or what's keeping you from corrective action?

Which do you believe keeps us placing "The cart before the horse" our being impatient with the process, extremely zealous, or having such a fear of failing that we begin performing not to fail as opposed to performing to succeed?

Which of these is your weak point and how do you intend to overcome that hurdle?

Is there a difference between thinking of preventative measures and thinking "How can I not to fail"?

Define the difference. Write the difference out and then Act Accordingly to experience your Expected Outcome.

Our perception can be a tool for building opportunity or a weapon that can destroy opportunity.

Matthew 6:11
International Standard Version
Give us today our daily bread,

Do you look for the silver lining or do you only see the dark clouds? Often times we unknowingly commit suicide when it comes to our favor, blessings, and abundance. How so? Being a complainer and being stubborn are the quickest ways of doing so.

True story, while working for this food courier company I ran into issues with this particular restaurant. I didn't want to carry the hot bag into a particular restaurant that required it because it was an inconvenience for me. The bag was a large bag. I didn't want to waste the trip so I decided I'll just comply. Complaining, I returned to my car thinking how unreasonable their requirement was and determined that I was not going to accept orders for that location again because of their preference. While en route to deliver I received a text from the customer stating that once I delivered the order to their carport there would be an additional tip for me on the table.

I immediately thought about my actions and my words and thought of how I could have potentially lost out on not just future pay for service but additional pay as well.

Be careful about stubbornness when it comes to what God requires. Be careful of complaining about what is a slight inconvenience momentarily. God may very well be placing us in a position not only of favor and blessing but also with additional measure attached.

#ActAccordingly

DAY 23

Journal

Our perception can be a tool for building opportunity or a weapon that can destroy opportunity.

Matthew 6:11
International Standard Version
Give us today our daily bread,

Have you ever come across a certain tool or object in your home again and again and thoughtlessly move it to any random place and once a moment of needing it arrives you absolutely could not recall the last location you placed it in?

How many relationships can you recall that you have handled in this same fashion?

Why do you believe when we become accustomed to having something provided for us or having a person or people as constants in our lives we tend to place much less importance on their importance to us over time?

Why does our appreciation depreciate?

Did you have a high level of appreciation and value for your job when you were first hired? Did it provide income for your bills to be paid?

Did it provide income for your wants and entertainment? Does it still do all those things presently?

So the job didn't change. What has changed is your level of appreciation and value for what you held in high importance once you now view it as something common?

It isn't possible to do addition, subtraction, multiplication and so on if you do not first learn numbers and their value placement.

Would you then agree or disagree that every prior stage remains as relevant as every stage that will follow?

Matthew 6:11
International Standard Version
Give us today our daily bread,

Have you ever considered what the full spectrum of our daily bread is? All that is included in that passage?

(Our food, clothing, shelter, means of income, allowing our involuntary body functions to perform without difficulty, no loss of a loved one throughout the night, amongst the many other daily allowances that we continue receiving.)

Answer this question. When do we begin to be thankful for the things we take for granted the most?

Which of these do you believe prompts God to give us more than just our daily bread?

A.   *A consistent appreciation and expression of gratitude for what we have while waiting for more?*

B.   *A continual attitude of complaint about how this is not enough or good enough and how I need the upgrade of this because I do not like this one any longer so I want more, better, or a different one?*

Final Answer?

Do you presently match your response?

If you believe you need more of the personality of choice "A" how do you intend to implement

STARTING THIS DAY to practice being that?

DAY 24
Devotional

There are many who go no further than visits to their dreams. Then there are the few that live to experience their dreams.

Hebrews 11:1
Living Bible
What is faith? It is the confident assurance that something we want is going to happen. It is the certainty that what we hope for is waiting for us, even though we cannot see it up ahead.

The "What" and the "Why" are primary in Belief and Faith. They have everything to do with what we anticipate receiving and what we expect to receive. The two words seem at a glance very much similar but anticipation and expectation tend to differ when it comes to spiritual matters. Anticipation has a slight open window of "if" or "perhaps" when looking towards a particular outcome occurring. There are many variables that could easily alter the outlook of what we may anticipate.

Expectation has an assurance attached to its ending. There's a certainty in the process towards seeing that projected outcome take place.

Anticipation often leads to disappointment because of the many variables that must be in harmony in order to bring a desired outcome to reality. Especially the human variable. That is the variable that floats and isn't certain.

Now when we are placing our trust in God, there is an assured certainty that what we are looking forward to will be. God is faithful to His promises and there are no questionable that are outside of His control. In fact, God is the architect and what He designs is flawless.

Faith isn't simply a matter of trusting God but that we're placing our trust in God.

#ActAccordingly

DAY 24
Journal

There are many who go no further than visits to their dreams. Then there are the few that live to experience their dreams.

Hebrews 11:1
Living Bible
What is faith? It is the confident assurance that something we want is going to happen. It is the certainty that what we hope for is waiting for us, even though we cannot see it up ahead.

Would you consider yourself a person who lives according to faith or by whatever is meant to happen will happen?

How did this come about?

I believe that most of the population limit the practice of faith to only having relation to

God and spiritual matters. Which is far from correct.

Truthfully we are operating by faith in multiple instances on a daily basis.

Faith in our alarms waking us at the designated hour, that chairs we sit in will support our weight, and an even greater use of faith is after working a 40 or 80 hour work period having a high certainty we will be compensated for our efforts afterwards.

We believe our days are going to respond to how we speak them and then we proceed forward in conjunction with those expectations becoming realities yet to be experienced.

(Refer again to Hebrews 11:1)

Why do we offer less resistance when it comes to placing our faith in persons, systems, and objects and greater resistance when needing to place our faith in God the creator of all persons and things?

Do you struggle with faith itself or just placing faith in something outside of our control? What makes it a struggle?

When someone wants to become a lawyer they don't just desire to be a lawyer and one day suddenly awake as a lawyer. There is a belief in something to help make that decision possible, the appropriate courses to be completed, and a final testing to obtain the recognition of esquire. Dreams and expectations require activities to ensure those dreams move from intangible thoughts to tangible experiences.

Faith requires the same currency exchange.

The larger the expected outcome the larger the level of faith must also be. There is our part and there is God's.

How often have circumstances changed in your favor that you could not control? Who did you give the credit to?

How many times did certain opportunities reveal themselves to you without any participation from you?

Who did you give credit to?

Realizing that faith isn't just believing but believing fully and taking appropriate activity, how do you intend to now view what is larger than what you can control the outcome of?

DAY 25
Devotional

Willingly going the "Extra Mile" is a matter of devotion to the purpose.

Luke 22:42

J.B. Phillips New Testament

—"Father, if you are willing, take this cup away from me—but it is not my will, but yours, that must be done."

Foundations are non-negotiable when it comes to the construction or formation of anything. Healthy relationships can only be sustained from being built upon a foundation of trust. Mutual happiness will not be experienced without it. Teams - whether in business or sports - can only excel when there has been a foundation of trust and cooperation established. Championships or milestones will not be achieved without the presence of cohesiveness. All parts must function together for the benefit of the whole. No person can be an individual when attempting to accomplish the larger goal. As the larger goal is being met individual goals also get accomplished.

So it is also in our walking with our Lord God. God is always extending Himself towards us and for us. Actually, God has been from before creation establishing his faithfulness to us. It would be safe to say, He has created a history of showing that He is to be trusted. God isn't just faithful, He is Faithfulness. In essence, God has no need of practicing to become what He is composed of.

God has as much concern for our future successes and desires as we do. In fact, He's so vested in our successes and desires He made a plan for those very experiences to be ours. (Jeremiah 29:11)

Our cooperation and willingness to be a contributor to the Kingdom of heaven will literally put us, us as in God and ourselves, in a position of together always encountering victories and triumphs.

#ActAccordingly

DAY 25
Journal

Willingly going the "Extra Mile" is a matter of devotion to the purpose.

Luke 22:42
J.B. Phillips New Testament
—*"Father, if you are willing, take this cup away from me—but it is not my will, but yours, that must be done."*

Losing unhealthy weight requires the discipline of healthy eating practices. Excelling in academics requires discipline and attentiveness to study practices.

Which usually drives you to accomplish tasks that require much from you, the benefits of its completion or the completion of it simply for the reward?

Would you agree or disagree that having a resilient "Why" increases the depth of your devotion to an undertaking more than being emotionally excited about one?

Which of the two do you regularly perform from?

Is there a difference only between the two approaches to the process or are there also differences in the outcomes and if so what are the differences?

Which end of the spectrum do you fall when tasks begin to morph from being an enjoyable activity to becoming a task that places a demand on your resolve to finish, are you a "Closer" or a "Quitter"?

"Closers" will always choose accepting the challenge and finishing while "Quitters" will always choose excuses over completion. Draw a definitive line in the sand as to which you are today and live it out.

As of (*Today's date*) / (*Your name*) will always (*finish according to your personality type*)...

DAY 26
Devotional

Your next opportunity for growth may be a conversation with you not as the listener instead of the speaker.

Proverbs 27:17
Contemporary English Version
Just as iron sharpens iron, friends sharpen the minds of each other. In your opinion, what's the first principle rule in learning and why?

Who learns less in a one-sided conversation and why are their learning curves lessened? Once you become a teacher are you no longer a student? Why do you believe so?

Let's talk about social circles.

How many circles are you part of that exhilarates you yet intimidates you simultaneously? What is it about this circle that attributes to you feeling this way?

If you feel a certain level of comfort within one social setting you more than likely feel in one's element with the others. Why would this be?

Students are listeners. Teachers are also students that continue to listen. Know-it-alls aren't listeners because they enjoy hearing themselves.

Honest assessment: which category defines your listening capacity if you are a listener and what happens today if you intend to not only receive wisdom but share as well?

DAY 26
Journal

Your next opportunity for growth may be a conversation with you as the listener instead of the speaker.

Proverbs 27:17
Contemporary English Version
Just as iron sharpens iron, friends sharpen the minds of each other.

Ever been in the midst of a discussion that seemed to be above your expertise?

What about listening in on a discussion and you wanted to contribute but you had no experience or knowledge to add any input?

I've been there on more than one occasion. My insecurity led me to avoid certain social gatherings or just walk away from the discussions I couldn't contribute to. Why? I didn't want to feel inadequate and not as smart as those I was listening to. I later discovered some information that changed my outlook. What I discovered was that no one knows more than another or is more intelligent than another. There are just subjects that interest one person more than another so they do their research and acquire information. This is the only reason why it would appear that one person seems to be much smarter than another. They're informed and knowledgeable about subjects that matter to them.

That feeling of inadequacy had I not corrected it would have not only continued to hold my potential hostage but place a cover over the reservoir of the information I contain. Recipients receive. Recipients don't give, they receive.

Miscommunication, misunderstanding, and in some cases, "I didn't know" can all be solved by less speaking and more listening.

#ActAccordingly

DAY 27
Devotional

External factors are not our triumph or defeat determiners. Our discipline of response or recklessness of reaction leads us to the one or to the other.

Revelation 3:2
New Life Version
Wake up! Make stronger what you have before it dies.

Why do we continue to view goals as something that must be conquered? Goals don't possess any power to be resistant toward us or cooperative with us. In fact, take notice of this. Goals are inanimate tangibles that can always be obtained so long as our devotion to experiencing a desired result is absolute and non-negotiable. Our decision to continue until our expectations are achieved or not finishing what we began always rests squarely upon no one's shoulders but our own. Repeat this statement. **Any defeat or triumph I experience is always a result of me, _____** *(place your name).*

Never have I heard anyone with high levels of excitement say to themselves, "I can't wait to get discouraged and quit in the middle of _____ (you fill in the blank with a goal), I just can't wait!"

Whenever you place a goal or an expectation before yourself, understand that it is going to be the pattern of old practices that you must conquer in order to realize the next progressive version of yourself.

That is what requires conquering! What requires conquering is that part of you that is unable and unwilling to take you into grasping your desired you. Whatever is undisciplined in you in regards to your next achievement is the opponent you must conquer. Stop looking around for someone to go up against. That someone that daily looks back at you through the mirror is who you must always go up against. Defeat that undisciplined reflection. It isn't the goal that you want to crush, it's your undiscipline that you want conquered.

#ActAccordingly

DAY 27
Journal

External factors are not our triumph or defeat determiners. Our discipline of responses or recklessness of reaction lead us to the one or to the other.

Revelation 3:2
New Life Version
Wake up! Make stronger what you have before it dies.

During the mid 1980s to early 90s there was a popular television series *MacGyver* whose main character always found a way out of impossible life and death situations on this show. MacGyver could gather ordinary objects from wherever he was trapped and with some creative scientific principles triumph over what should have been a hopeless outcome.

MacGyver was unwilling to believe he was trapped or beaten so he would work with what was available to defy the odds.

Are you one of those "Under different circumstances I could have…" or "If I only had this resource or knew the right people I could have…" types?

Why do we place so much more emphasis on these elements being the nucleus to our successes more than we place on ourselves?

Who in your opinion would be the first to receive opportunity's visit first, the person attempting to go straight to the benefits of an opportunity or the person working through the process for an appointment with opportunity?

Comparison is a crippler and disabler of destinies because it keeps us looking at what we don't have as a handicap and what we do have as too feeble to build on.

Success really isn't contingent on finding the right opportunity but rather having our abilities ready to merge with the availability of different resources to enhance what we already have. Start realizing you're the opportunity! Present yourself as the opportunity!

Does knowing you're the opportunity change your view of accomplishment? How do you now intend to change your winning percentage numbers?

Value isn't determined by "What you have" but "What you are".

Proverbs 22:29

New American Bible (Revised Edition)

Do you see those skilled at their work? They will stand in the presence of kings, but not in the presence of the obscure.

There's a saying often used in expressing the recognition of similar qualities between individuals that goes, "Real recognizes real, and you're looking real familiar."

This statement is commonly used in relation to offering a compliment between achievers and then we have the reality of there also being the other side of a coin. Needless to say, this statement could be used in regards to qualities of excellence as well as the qualities of mediocrity.

If you are unsure of how to distinguish where you would be weighted most heavily on this spectrum of excellence and mediocrity I will offer this suggestion. Ask yourself this question. Dwell on it before answering it with full honesty. Would you be honored or offended if others viewed you as possessing or exhibiting the same characteristics of the top five individuals you socialize with most frequently?

Continuing to be the smartest person in the group isn't being smart. Continuing to be the most accomplished person in the group will eventually lead to a diminishing of pursuing greater. It is coded into our DNA to create standards and not to simply meet standards. That means there is something that is so "You specific" that it cannot be replicated. An unusual excellence in the very details of how you do and accomplish. Being a candidate isn't being your most excellent. Being a candidate is being of the ability level as someone else.

Don't ever be in the "Birds of a feather flock together" crowd but rather the "Eagles fly alone" because they are unlike the other species of birds. Set yourself apart by a theme of excellence.

#ActAccordingly

DAY 28
Journal

Value isn't determined by "What you have" but "What you are".

Proverbs 22:29
New American Bible (Revised Edition)
Do you see those skilled at their work? They will stand in the presence of kings, but not in the presence of the obscure.

Which carries greater significance? What we do or how we perform what we do and why does one carry greater impact than the other?

When it comes to the matter of consistency, would you prefer a person of excellence or a person who can do excellent?

What difference was influential in your decision?

Between the choices of excellence and excellent, which end of the scale do you find yourself? ***(SOMEWHERE IN THE MIDDLE IS NOT OPTIONAL OR ACCEPTABLE)***

Which individual would you prefer in a customer service experience, the individual of excellence or the individual that knows how to do excellent and why is that your choice?

Are your interactions with others a mirror of what you yourself expect to receive from others or do you operate with a double standard in the transaction of giving and receiving with others? EXAMPLE: Is your being courteous and respectful based on your mood at that moment or do you remain courteous and respectful regardless of a mood?

Where do you know you need to be better and what plan of action should you follow to do so in order for you to grow into a person of excellence?

(HINT: Putting it in writing makes it a commitment.)

DAY 29
Devotional

Moving prematurely could prove to be more costly than moving incorrectly.

Ecclesiastes 10:10
New Living Translation
A dull ax requires great strength, so sharpen the blade. That's the value of wisdom; it helps you succeed.

There is always a Strategic Pattern (SP) that must be implemented in whatever we intend to go forward in. Everything we intend to move forward in is required to have an SP. Cooking, dieting, shopping, construction, vacations. All of these things seem random but they all require a prior preparation before you can actually engage in any of them.

I'll give you evidence now. Before you began reading this entry didn't you envision yourself doing so? You saw where you would be seated and how much time you would spend meditating on what you read before concluding the moment.

Actions without an SP end up becoming attempts not efforts that will not yield an intended result. Why? There was no strategy implemented, just reaction and excitement void of a process to deliver that desired result. This type of action comes with a burden of corrective requirements prior to proceeding forward again. Time mismanagement and energy misdirection doesn't have to always end with a consequence of a derailment. Prior preparation processes won't prolong your timetable of success but rather ensure the inevitability of it.

#ActAccordingly

DAY 29
Journal

Moving prematurely could prove to be more costly than moving incorrectly.

Ecclesiastes 10:10
New Living Translation
Using a dull ax requires great strength, so sharpen the blade. That's the value of wisdom; it helps you succeed.

What would you consider to be the largest reason we rush into matters prematurely? Why are mistakes simpler to correct than spontaneous actions?

Are you aware that decisions led by excitement could actually result in consequence rather than reward and benefit?

How do you think a consequence could possibly result from pursuing a great idea?

Definition of Reckless:
Acting or done with a lack of care or caution; careless or irresponsible.

When was the last time you took off impulsively from excitement with an idea and no formed strategy and it turned as expected? Extremely few and between?

This is what happens when there is no Plan of Action before going into action.

We cannot dictate the precise outcome of every undertaking but we can lessen the probability of disappointment considerably by formation of action steps.

What practice can you implement as of today to decrease the probability of disappointment within your life's choices and also remain constant in it?

DAY 30
Devotional

Once we start trusting us, our abilities begin trusting us.

Exodus 4:2
New Living Translation
Then the Lord asked him, "What is that in your hand?"

The staff that Moses carried turned out to have far greater usefulness than just the common use of directing sheep or being a walking stick. It would seem that Moses was in possession of something that God intended to use and demonstrate as having far greater value than Moses realized at various moments.

We have all experienced at some point whether it was under pressure or just because opportunity saw fit to be available, something we already possessed be exposed as this wonder of the world. We tend to always view other individuals as possessors of extraordinary skills and almost never view ourselves through that same lens. Here's the truth: all they did was pursue interest in a particular area and then further decided to seek a higher standard of performance for themselves within that area.

There's absolutely no difference between there being things that only you can do in the way that only you can do them and there being things that others can do in the way that only they can do them. There's no difference except the difference we decide to make between ourselves and them. That difference is the existence or the deficit of your **Confidence** in you. The capacity of the level of excellence you perform at solely depends on your confidence level.

#ActAccordingly

DAY 30
Journal

Once we start trusting us, our abilities begin trusting us.

Exodus 4:2
New Living Translation
Then the Lord asked him, "What is that in your hand?"

I believe many things we attempt for the first time will always seem beyond our ability at an initial glance. Yet once that technique surfaces that ignites our confidence it's straightforward and no turning back.

How much value do you currently place on who you are and your abilities?

As of now are you aware of all that you are capable of and have the capacity to perform?

POTENTIAL

A latent excellence or ability that may or may not be developed.

Recognizing the opportunity to turn your potential into an ability is more consequential than the opportunity itself. What about this statement do you find agreement with and why or what do you perhaps disagree with and why?

Which are resources? Which are tools?

A. Tangible objects such as money, data, and correct associations
B. Possessing the ability to create new or better and a willingness to discipline ourselves to form even more productive practices

Which would you consider resources and which would you consider tools and why? Which is most vital to trust to deliver your expectations in life, an opportunity or yourself?

Trusting in yourself is paramount.

What will you implement as of today to show yourself you trust you in the pursuit to release your potential?

Would you consider the conflict of us wanting to have what's good to us over what would be best for us one of the greater underlying reasons we experience disappointment?

What is usually the primary cause you experience disappointment?

When you do experience disappointment do you approach it with gaining perspective, being insistent on pursuing your preference, or do you sulk in feeling defeated

Printed in the United States
by Baker & Taylor Publisher Services